The Verse of Lichtenstein

Alfred Lichtenstein

Alpha Editions

This edition published in 2024

ISBN : 9789362922014

Design and Setting By
Alpha Editions
www.alphaedis.com
Email - info@alphaedis.com

As per information held with us this book is in Public Domain.
This book is a reproduction of an important historical work. Alpha Editions uses the best technology to reproduce historical work in the same manner it was first published to preserve its original nature. Any marks or number seen are left intentionally to preserve its true form.

I

Because I believe that many do not understand the verse of Lichtenstein, do not correctly understand, do not clearly understand—

II

The first eighty poems are lyric. In the usual sense. They are not much different from poetry that praises gardens. The content is the distress of love, death, universal longing. The impulse to formulate them in the "cynical" vein (like cabaret songs) may, for example, might have arisen from the wish to feel superior. Most of the eighty poems are insignificant. They were not presented to the public. All except one (one of the last) That is:

> I want to bury myself in the night,
> Naked and shy.
> And to wrap darknesses around my limbs
> And warm luster.
> I want to wander far behind the hills of the earth.
> Deep beyond the gliding oceans.
> Past the singing winds.
> There I'll meet the silent stars.
> They carry space through time.
> And live at the death of being.
> And among them are gray,
> Isolated things.
> Faded movement
> Of worlds long decayed.
> Lost sound.
> Who can know that.
> My blind dream watches far from earthly wishes.

III

The following poems can be divided into three groups. One combines fantastic, half-playful images: The Sad Man, Rubbers, Capriccio, The Patent-Leather Shoe, A Barkeeper's Coarse Complaint. (First appeared in Aktion, in Simplicissimus, in March, Pan and elsewhere). Pleasure in what is purely artistic is unmistakable.

Examples: The Athlete: in the background is a demonstration of a view of the world. The Athlete... means that it is terrible that a man must also intellectually move his bowels.—Rubbers: a man wearing rubbers is different without them.

IV

The earliest poetry forms a second group:

Twilight

The intention is to eliminate the difference between time and space in favor of the idea of poetry. The poems want to represent the effect of twilight on the landscape.

In this case the unity of time is necessary to a certain degree. The unity of space is not required, therefore not observed. In twelve lines the twilight is represented on a pond, tree, field, somewhere... its effect on the appearance of a young man, a wind, a sky, two cripples, a poet, a horse, a lady, a man, a young boy, a woman, a clown, a baby-carriage, some dogs is represented visually. (The expression is poor, but I can find nothing better)

The author of the poem does not want to portray a landscape that is thought to be real. The poetic art has the advantage over painting of offering "ideal" images. That means—in respect to the Twilight: the fat boy who uses the big pond as a toy, and the two cripples on crutches in the field and the woman on the city street who was knocked down by a cart-horse in the half-darkness, and the poet who, filled with desperate longing, is thinking in the evening (probably looking through a skylight), and the circus clown in the gray rear building who is sighing as he puts on his boots in order to arrive punctually at the performance, in which he must be funny—all these can produce a poetic "picture," although they cannot be composed like a painting. Most still deny that, and for that reason recognize, for example, in the "Twilight" and similar pictures nothing but a mindless confusion of strange performances. Others believe, incorrectly, that these kinds of "ideal" pictures are possible in painting (for example, the Futurist mish mash).

The intention, furthermore, to grasp the reflex of things directly—without superfluous reflections. Lichtenstein knows that the man is not stuck to the window, but stands behind it. That the baby-carriage is not screaming, but the child in the baby-carriage. Because he can only see the baby-carriage, he writes: the baby-carriage cries. It would have been untrue lyrically had he written: a man stands behind a window.

By chance, it is conceptually also not untrue: a boy plays with a pond. A horse stumbles over a lady. Dogs swear. Certainly one must laugh in an odd way when one learns to see: that a boy actually uses a pond as a toy. How horses have a helpless way of stumbling... how human dogs express their rage...

Sometimes the representation of reflection is important. Perhaps a poet goes mad—makes a deeper impression than—a poet stares stiffly ahead—

Something else compelling in the poem: fear and things that resemble reflection, like: all men must die... or: I am only a little book of pictures... that will not be discussed here.

V

That Twilight and other poems take things strangely (The comic is experienced tragically. The representation is "grotesque"), to notice the unbalanced, incoherent nature of things, arbitrariness, confusion... is not, in any case, the characteristic of "style." Proof is: Lichtenstein writes poems in which the "grotesque" disappears, without notice, behind the "ungrotesque."

Other differences between older poems (for example, Twilight) and later ones (for example, Fear) in the same style are detectable. One might observe that ever increasing idiosyncratic reflections about landscape clearly break through. Certainly not without artistic purpose.

VI

The third group consists of the poems of Kuno Kohn.

Alfred Lichtenstein

(Wilmersdorf)

The Athlete

> A man walked back and forth in his torn slippers
> In the small room
> He inhabited.
> He thought about the events
> About which he was informed by the evening paper.
> And sadly yawned, the way only that man yawns
> Who has read much that is strange—
> And the thought suddenly overcame him,
> Like a timid person who gets gooseflesh,
> And the way the person who stuffs himself
> Starts to burp,
> Like a mother in labor:
> The great yawn might perhaps be a sign,
> A nod from fate,
> To lie down to rest.
> And the thought would not leave him.
> And then he began to undress...
> When he was stark naked, he lifted something.

Rubbers

The fat man thought:
In the evening I gladly walk in rubbers,
But also when the streets are clean and spotless.
I am never entirely sober in rubbers.
I hold the cigarette in my hand.
My soul skips in little rhythms.
And all one hundred pounds of my body skips.

The Patent-leather Shoe

The poet thought: ah, I have enough trash!
The whores, the theater, and the moon in the city,
The dress-shirts, the streets, and smells,
The nights and the coaches and the windows,
The laughter, the street-lights and murders—
I'm really fed up now with all the crap,
Damn it!
Whatever will be will be—it's all the same to me:
The patent leather shoe Hurts me. And I take it off—
People might turn around, surprised.
Only it's a shame about my silk socks…

Smoke on the Field

Lene Levi went out in the evening,
Mincing, her skirt bunched up,
Through the long, empty streets
Of a suburb.

And she spoke weeping, aching, crazy,
Strange words,
Which the wind tossed, so that they popped,
Like pods.

They made bloody scratches on trees,
And, shredded, hung on houses
And in these deaf streets
died all alone.

Lene Levi went out, until all
The roofs made their crooked mouths grimace,
And the windows and the shadows
Made faces

They had a completely drunken good time—
Until the houses became helpless
And the mute city passed

Into the broad fields,
Which the moon smeared…

Little Lene took out of her pocket
A box of cigarettes,
Weeping took one
Out and smoked.

Dreaming

Paul said:

Ah, but who wouldn't want to drive a car forever—
We burrow our way through high-stemmed woods,
We pass by spaces that seem endless.
We pass through the wind and attack the towns, which speed up.
But the odors of the sluggish cities are hateful to us—
Ah, we are flying! Always alongside death…
How we despise and scorn him who sits on our lives!
Who lays out graves for us and makes all streets crooked—ha, we laugh at him,
and the roads, overcome, die with us—
Thus we shall auto our way through the whole world…
Until, on some clear evening
We find a violent ending against a sturdy tree.

The Sad Man

No, I have no capacity for life.
I could be considered foolish—
Today I am not going to the restaurant.
I am after all this time weary of the waiters,
Who scornfully bring us, with their smug grimaces,
Dark beer and make us so confused
That we cannot find our home
And we must
Use the foolish street lights
To prop ourselves up
with weak hands.
Today I have bigger things in mind—
Ah, I shall find out the meaning of existence.
And in the evening I shall do some roller skating
Or go at some point to Temple.

Capriccio

Here is the way I shall die:
It's dark. And it has rained.
But you can no longer detect the imprint of the clouds
Which up there cover the sky in soft silk.
All streets are flowing, black mirrors,
Over the piled up houses, where streetlights,
Strings of pearls, hang shining.
And high above thousands of stars are flying,
Silver insects, around the world—
I am among them. Somewhere.
And sunken, I watch very seriously, somewhat pale,
But rather thoughtful about the refined, heavenly blue legs of a lady,
While an auto cuts me to pieces, so that my head rolls like a red marble
At her feet...
She is surprised. And swears like a lady. And kicks it
Haughtily with the dainty heel
Of her little shoe
Into the gutter.

The Turk

A totally perverse Turk bought for himself,
Out of grief for the recent death
Of plump Fatme, his favorite wife,
From his white-slaver, two former mannequins, in quite good condition—
You could almost say: brand new—
Just imported from France.
When he had them, he sang, in celebration of himself:

Sit down on my thighs.
Hold me around my loins.
With your sweet tongues
Stroke my tearful cheeks.
Ah, you have such beautifully bejeweled
Eyes and such clear hands,
Weariest of my wives,
And such long, gentle legs.
Tomorrow I buy six pairs of new
Stockings of the thinnest silk
As well as very small, black silk shoes.
And in the evening you will dance
Soft, false dances

In the new silk shoes
And new silk stockings.
In the garden. In the sun.
Close to the water.
But at night I'll have you whipped
By four smiling eunuchs.

Hugo von Hofmannsthal's Barber

I stand this way on cloudy winter days
From dawn to dusk and I soap heads,
Shave them and powder them and speak
Indifferent words, stupid, foolish.
Most heads are completely shut,
They sleep limply. And others read again
And look slowly through long lids,
As though they had sucked everything dry.
Still others open the red cracks of their mouths wide
And tell jokes.
For my part, I smile courteously. Ah, I hide
Deep under these smiles, as though in a coffin,
The terrible, repressed, wise complaints
About the fact that we are forced into this existence,
Jammed in, firmly and inescapably trapped
As though in jail, and we wear chains,
Confusing, hard, that we do not understand.
And the fact that each man is distant and estranged from himself
As though from a neighbor whom he does not know at all,
And whose house he has always only seen from the outside.
Sometimes, when I am shaving a chin,
Knowing that a whole life
Is in my power, that I am now master,
I, a barber, and that a missed stroke,
A slice too deep, cuts off the round, cheerful head
That lies before me (he is thinking of a woman,
Books, business) from his body,
As though it were a loose button on a vest—
I am overcome. Then the feeling came over me... this animal.
Is there. The animal... both my knees knock.
And like a small boy tearing paper
Without knowing why,
And like students who kill gas lamps,
And like children who turn so red
When they tear the wings of captured flies,

So I would like to do the same,
As if it were a slip,
To make a scratch with my knife on such a chin.
I would too gladly watch the red stream of blood spray.

Spring

A certain Rudolf called out:
I have eaten too much.
Whether it's healthy is very questionable.
After such a greasy lunch
I really feel uncomfortable.
But I belch beautifully and smoke
Cigarettes now and then.
Lying on my heavy belly,
I chirp nothing but songs of spring.
Longingly, as though on a ramp
The voice squeals from the throat.
And like an old lamp
The wind blackens the bitter soul.

A Barkeeper's Coarse Complaint

It's enough to make me throw the chair through the panes of the mirror Into the street—
There I sit with raised eyebrows:
All bars are full,
My bar is empty—isn't that terrific...
Isn't that strange... isn't that enough to make you puke,,,
The damned jerks—the miserable phonies—
Everyone goes right by me...
Bloody mess...
Here I am burning gas and electricity—
May God and the devil damn me to hell:
Damn It all... why is my bar the only empty one...
Grumpy, reproachful waiters standing around—
It is my fault—
Not one damned person comes to the door—
Cramped in a corner I sit with a hopeful face.
No customers come.—
The food rots, the wine and bread.
I might as well shut the joint.
And cry myself to death.

A Trouble-making Girl

It's certainly late. I must earn something.
But they're all going right by today with smug expressions on their
faces.
They don't want to give me a single good-luck penny.
It's a miserable life.
If I come home without money
The old lady will throw me out.
There is hardly anyone on the street any more.
I am dead tired and freezing.
I was never so miserable in my life.
I move around here like a piece of meat.
Finally someone comes over:
An extremely well-dressed man—
But in this life one can't tell much
By appearances.
He's also quite older. (they have more money,
Young ones tend to cheat you.)
We are face-to-face.
I raise my clothes above the knee.
I can get away with that.
That's the big draw..
Like flies to the light
The guys are drawn to us goats...
The John is certainly standing over there.
He is staring. He winks. Now I'll go right by him...
I think: he will give me a big piece of gold.
Then I get drunk in secret on expensive liquor,
That's still the best: sometime—alone
To be drunk quietly, for myself—
Or I can buy new shoes...
I won't have to go around in mended socks—
Or... sometime I won't go out walking the streets.
And take a rest from the guys—
Or... I'm already looking forward to this...
I'm so happy—
Here comes Kitty.
And scares the man off.

The Drunkard

One must guard oneself ever so carefully against
Howling, without any reason, like an animal.
Against pouring beer over the faces of all the waiters,
And kicking them in their faces.

Against shortening the disgusting time
Spent lying in a gutter.
Against throwing oneself off a bridge.
Against hitting friends in the mouth.
Against suddenly, while dogs bark,
Tearing the clothes off a well-fed body.
Against hurling into any old beloved woman's
Thighs one's dark skull.

A Lieutenant General Sings

I am the Division Commander,
His Excellency.
I have attained what is humanly possible.
A lovely consciousness.
In front of me
Important people and chiefs of regiments
Bend their knees,
And my generals
Obey my commands.
God willing, my next command will be
An entire military corps.
Women, drama, music
Do not interest me much.
Compared to parades and battles,
That does not amount to much.
Would that there were an endless war
With bloody, howling winds.
Ordinary life
Has no charm for me.

Falling in the River

Drunk, Lene Levi walked
In the neighboring streets nightly
Back and forth, screaming, "auto."
Her blouse was opened,
So that one saw her fine, fascinating
Underclothing and skin.
Seven horny little men ran
After Lene.

Seven horny little men chased
Lene Levi for her body,
Thinking about what it costs.
Seven men, otherwise very respectable,

Forgot their children and art,
Science and factory.
And they ran as though possessed
After Lene Levi.
Lene Levi stopped
On a bridge, catching her breath,
And she lifted her blurred blue
Drunken glances in the wide
Sweet darkness above
The street lamps and the houses.
Seven randy little men though
Caught Lene's eye.

Seven randy little men tried
To touch Lene Levi's heart.
Lene remained unapproachable.
Suddenly she jumped up on the railing,
Turns up her nose at the world for the last time,
Joyfully jumps into the river.
Seven pale little men ran,
As quickly as they could, out of the place.

A Poor Man Sings

Those were fine times, when I still
Walked in silk socks and wore underpants,
Sometimes had ten marks to spare, in order
To hire a woman, bored in the day
Night after night I sat in the coffeehouse.
Often I was so sated that I
Did not know what to order for myself.

Twilight

A fat young man plays with a pond.
The wind has caught itself in a tree.
The pale sky seems to be rumpled,
As though it had run out of makeup.
On long crutches, bent nearly in half
And chatting, two cripples creep across the field.
A blond poet perhaps goes mad.
A little horse stumbles over a lady.
A fat man is stuck to a window.
A boy wants to visit a soft woman.
A gray clown puts on his boots.
A baby carriage shrieks and dogs curse.

The Night

    Sleepy policemen waddle under streetlights.
    Broken beggars grumble when they sense people.
    On some corners powerful streetcars stutter.
    And plush cabs drop into the stars.
    Among rough houses whores hobble back and forth,
    Sadly swinging their ripe behinds.
    Much sky lies broken in these dried-out things…
    Whiny cats painfully shriek bright songs.

The Cabaret in the Suburbs

    The sweaty heads of waiters tower above the room
    Like lofty and powerful capitals.
    Lice-ridden boys giggle nastily.
    And shining girls give painfully beautiful looks.
    And distant women are so very excited…
    They have hundreds of red, round hands,
    Still, large, without end
    Placed around their high, motley bellies.
    Most people are drinking yellow beer.
    Grocers, their cigarettes burning, gape.
    A fine young woman sings vulgar songs.
    A young Jew plays the piano with great pleasure.

The Trip to the Mental Hospital

    Fat trains go down loud tracks
    Past houses, which are like coffins.
    On the corners wheelbarrows with bananas squat.
    Just a bit of shit makes a tough kid happy.
    The human beasts glide along, completely lost
    As though on a street, miserably gray and shrill.
    Workers stream from dilapidated gates.
    A weary person moves quietly in a round tower.
    A hearse crawls along the street, two steeds out front,
    Soft as a worm and weak.
    And over all lies an old rag—
    The sky… pagan and meaningless.

Into the Evening

    Out of crooked clouds priceless things grow.
    Very tiny things suddenly become important.
    The sky is green and opaque
    Down there where the blind hills glide.

Tattered trees stagger into the distance.
Drunken meadows spin in a circle,
And all the surfaces become gray and wise…
Only villages crouch glowingly: red stars—

Interior

A large space—half dark… deadly… completely confused…
Provocative!… delicate… dream-like… recesses, heavy doors
And broad shadows, which lead to blue corners…
And somewhere a sound that clinks like a Champagne glass.
On a fragile rug lies a wide picture book,
Distorted and exaggerated by a green ceiling light.
How—soft little cats—piously white girls make love!
In the background an old man and a silk handkerchief.

Morning

… And all the streets lie smooth and shining there.
Only occasionally does a solid citizen hurry along them.
A swell girl argues violently with Papa.
A baker happens to be looking at the lovely sky.
The dead sun, wide and thick, hangs on the houses.
Four fat wives screech in front of a bar.
A carriage driver falls and breaks his neck.
And everything is boringly bright, healthy and clear.
A gentleman with wise eyes hovers, confused, in the dark,
A failing god… in this picture, that he forgot,
Perhaps did not notice—he mutters this and that. Dies. And laughs.
Dreams of a stroke, paralysis, osteoporosis.

Landscape

(for a picture)
With all its branches a slender tree casts
The shine of darkness around poor crosses.
The earth stretches out painfully black and broad.
A small moon slips slowly out of space.
And next to it strange, unapproachable, huge
Airplanes hover heavenward!
Sinners filled with longing look up, with belief
And tear themselves out of their tombs.

The Concert

The naked seats hearken strangely
Alarming and quiet, as though there were some danger.

Only some are covered with a person.
A green girl often looks into a book.
And someone else finds a handkerchief.
And the boots are disgustingly encrusted.
A sound comes from an old man's open mouth.
A young boy looks at a young girl.
A boy plays with the button on his trousers.
On a podium an agile body rocks
To the rhythm of its serious instrument.
On a collar lies a shiny head.
Screeches. And tears.

Winter

A dog shrieks in misery from a bridge
To heaven... which stands like old gray stone
Upon far-off houses. And, like a rope
Made of tar, a dead river lies on the snow.
Three trees, black frozen flames, make threats
At the end of the earth. They pierce
With sharp knives the rough air,
In which a scrap of bird hangs all alone.
A few street lights wade towards the city,
Extinguished candles for a corpse. And a smear
Of people shrinks together and is soon
Drowned in the wretched white swamp.

The Operation

In the sunlight doctors tear a woman apart.
Here the open red body gapes. And heavy blood
Flows, dark wine, into a white bowl. One sees
Very clearly the rose-red cyst. Lead gray,
The limp head hangs down. The hollow mouth
Rattles. The sharp yellow chin points upward.
The room shines, cool and friendly. A nurse
Savors quite a bit of sausage in the background.

Cloudy Evening

The sky is swollen with tears and melancholy.
Only far off, where its foul vapors burst,
Green glow pours down. The houses,
Gray grimaces, are fiendishly bloated with mist.

Yellowish lights are beginning to gleam.
A stout father with wife and children dozes.

Painted women are practicing their dances.
Grotesque mimes strut towards the theater.

Jokers shriek, foul connoisseurs of men:
The day is dead... and a name remains!
Powerful men gleam in girls' eyes.
A woman yearns for her beloved woman.

Sunday Afternoon

Packs of houses squat along rotten streets,
Around whose hump a gray sun shines.
A perfumed, half crazy little poodle
Casts exhausted eyes at the big world.
In a window a boy catches flies.
A badly soiled baby gets angry.
On the horizon a train moves through windy meadows:
Slowly paints a long thick stroke.
Like typewriters hackney hooves clatter.
A dust-covered, noisy athletic club comes along.
Brutal shouts stream from bars for coachmen.
Yet fine bells mix with them.
On the fairgrounds where athletes wrestle,
Everything is dark and indistinct.
A barrel organ howls and scullery maids sing.
A man is smashing a rotting woman.

The Excursion

(Dedicated to Kurt Lubasch, July 15, 1912)

You, I can endure these stolid
Rooms and barren streets
And the red sun on the houses,
And the books read
A million times ago.
Come, we must go far
Away from the city.
Let us lie down
In this gentle meadow.
Let us raise, threatening yet helpless
Against the mindless, large,
Deadly blue, shiny skies,
The fleshless, dull eyes,
The cursed hands,
Swollen from crying.

Summer Evening

>All things are seamless,
>As though forgotten, light and dull.
>From the sacred heights the green sky spills
>Still water on the city.
>Glazed cobblers' lamps shine.
>Empty bakeries are waiting.
>People in the street, astonished, stride
>Towards a miracle.
>A copper red goblin runs
>Up towards the roof, up and down.
>Little girls fall, sobbing
>From the poles of street lights.

The Trip to the Mental Hospital (II)

>A little girl crouches with her little brother
>Next to an overturned barrel of water.
>In rags, a beast of a person lies gulping food
>Like a cigarette butt on the yellow sun.
>Two skinny goats stand in broad green spaces
>On pegs, and their ropes sometimes tighten.
>Invisible behind monstrous trees
>Unbelievably at peace the huge horror approaches.

Peace

>In weary circles a sick fish hovers
>In a pond surrounded by grass.
>A tree leans against the sky—burned and bent.
>Yes… the family sits at a large table,
>Where they peck with their forks from the plates.
>Gradually they become sleepy, heavy and silent.
>The sun licks the ground with its hot, poisonous,
>Voracious mouth, like a dog—a filthy enemy.
>Bums suddenly collapse without a trace.
>A coachman looks with concern at a nag
>Which, torn open, cries in the gutter.
>Three children stand around in silence.

Towards Morning

>What do I care about the swift newspaper boys.
>The approach of the late auto-beasts does not frighten me.
>I rest on my moving legs.
>My face is wet with rain.

Green remains of the night
Stick to my eyes.
That's the way I like it—
Even as the sharp, secret
Drops of water crack on thousands of walls.
Plop from thousands of roofs.
Hop along shining streets…
And all the sullen houses
Listen to their
Eternal song.
Close behind me the burning night is ruined…
Its smelly corpse burdens my back.
But above me I feel the rushing,
Cool heaven.
Behold—I am in front of a
Streaming church.
Large and quiet it takes me in.
Here I shall stay for a while.
Immersed in its dreams.
Dreams out of gray
Silk that does not shimmer.

Bad Weather

A frozen moon stands waxen,
White shadows,
Dead face,
Above me and the dull
Earth.
Throws green light
Like a garment,
A wrinkled one,
On bluish land.
But from the edge
Of the city,
Like a soft hand without fingers,
Gently rises
And fearfully threatening like death
Dark, nameless…
Rising
Without sound,
An empty slow sea swells towards us—
At first it was only like a weary
Moth, which crawled over the last houses.

Now it is a black bleeding hole.
It has already buried the city and half the sky.
Ah, had I flown—
Now it is too late.
My head falls into
Desolate hands.
On the horizon an apparition like a shriek
Announces
Terror and imminent end.

The Sick

Evening and grief and lamp light
Bury our death-face.

We sit at the window and drop out of it,
Far off day still squints at a gray house.
We scarcely touch our life…
And the world is a morphine dream…
Blinded by clouds the sky sinks.
The garden expires in dark wind—
The watchmen enter,
Lift us up into bed,
Inject us with poison,
Kill the lamp.
Curtains hang in front of the night…
They disappear gently and slowly—
Some groan, but no one speaks,
Our buried face sleeps.

Cloud

A fog has destroyed the world so gently.
Bloodless trees dissolve in smoke.
And shadows hover where shrieks are heard.
Burning beasts evaporate like breath.

Captured flies are the gas lanterns.
And each flickers, still attempting to escape.
But to one side, high in the distance, the poisonous moon,
The fat fog-spider, lies in wait, smoldering.

We, however, loathsome, suited for death,
Trample along, crunching this desert splendor.
And silently stab the white eyes of misery
Like spears into the swollen night.

The City

　　A white bird is the big sky.
　　Under it a cowering city stares.
　　The houses are half-dead old people.
　　A gaunt carriage-horse gapes grumpily.
　　Winds, skinny dogs, run weakly.
　　Their skins squeel on sharp corners.
　　In a street a crazed man groans: You, oh, you—
　　If only I could find you…
　　A crowd around him is surprised and grins derisively.
　　Three little people play blind man's bluff—
　　A gentle tear-stained god lays the grey powdery hands
　　Of afternoon over everything.

The World

(Dedicated to a clown)

　　Many days tread upon human animals,
　　In gentle oceans hunger-sharks fly.
　　Heads, beers glisten in coffee-houses.
　　Girls' screams shred on a man.
　　Thunderstorms come crashing down. Forest winds darken.
　　Women knead prayers in skinny hands:
　　May the Lord God send an angel.
　　A shred of moonlight shimmers in the sewers.
　　Readers of books crouch quietly on their bodies.
　　An evening dips the world in lilac lye.
　　The trunk of a body floats in a windshield.
　　From deep in the brain its eyes sink.

Prophecy

　　Some day—I have signs—a mortal storm
　　Is coming from the far north.
　　Everywhere is the smell of corpses.
　　The great killing begins.
　　The lump of sky grows dark,
　　Storm-death lifts its clawed paws;
　　All the lumps fall down,
　　Mimes burst. Girls explode.
　　Horses' stables crash to the ground.
　　Not a fly can escape.
　　Handsome homosexuals roll
　　Out of their beds.

The walls of houses develop fissures.
Fish rot in the stream.
Everything meets its own disgusting end.
Groaning buses tip over.

Winter Evening

Behind yellow windows shadows drink hot tea.
Yearning people sway on a hardened pond
Workers find a soft woman's corpse.
Glowing blue snows cast a howling darkness.
On high poles a scarecrow, implored, hangs.
Stores flicker dimly through frosted windows,
In front of which human bodies move like ghosts.
Students carve a frozen girl.
How lovely, the crystalline winter evening burning!
A platinum moon now streams through a gap in the houses.
Next to green lanterns under a bridge
Lies a gypsy woman. And plays an instrument.

Girls

They cannot stand their rooms in the evening.
They creep out into deep starry streets.

How gentle is the world in the streetlights' wind!
How strangely buzzing life melts away…
They go by gardens and houses,
As though very far off there might be a light,
And they look upon every horny man
As a sweet gentleman savior

After the Ball

Night creeps into the cellars, musty and dull.
Tuxedos totter through the rubble of the street.
Faces are moldy and worn out.
The blue morning burns coolly in the city.
How quickly music and dance and greed melted…
It smells of the sun. And day begins
With trolleys, horses, shouts and wind.
Dull daily labor cloaks the people in dust.
Families silently wolf down lunch.
At times a hall still vibrates through a skull,
Much dull desire and a silken leg.

Landscape

Like old bones in the pot
Of noon the damned streets lie there.
It's a long time since I saw you here.
A young man pulls at a girl's pigtail.
And a couple of dogs wallow in filth.
I would like to go arm and arm with you.
The sky is gray wrapping paper
On which the sun sticks—a spot of butter.

Moonscape

The yellow mother's eye burns up there.
Everywhere night lies like a blue cloth.
There is no question that I am sucking air.
I am only a little picture book.
Houses capture dreams of motley sleepers
As though in nets in the windows.
Autos creep like ladybugs
Up luminous streets.

Landscape in the Early Morning

The air is gray. Who knows something good for soot?
Next to an ox grazing on the ground
Stands an astonished deeply serious mountaineer.
Soon there is a powerful downpour of rain.
A young boy who is pissing on a meadow
Will be the source of a small river.
What should one do when nature calls!
Be natural. Be yourself.
A poet roams around in the world,
Observes for himself the orderly flow of traffic
And rejoices about sky, field, and dung.
Ah, and he takes careful notice of everything.
Then he climbs a high mountain
Which happens to be close by.

Return of the Village Boy

In my youth the world was a small pond,
Grandma and red roof, lowing
Of oxen and a clump of trees.
And all around the huge green meadow.
How lovely was this dreaming into distance.
This absolute nothingness as bright air and wind

And bird cries and fairy-tale books.
Far off the fabled iron snake whistled—

Summer Freshness

  The sky is like a blue jellyfish.
  And all around are fields, rolling meadows—
  Peaceful world, you great mousetrap,
  Would that I might finally escape from you.. O if I had wings—
  One plays dice. Guzzles. Chatters about future countries.
  Each person puts in his own two cents.
  The earth is a succulent Sunday roast,
  Nicely dunked into a sweet sun-sauce.
  If only there were a wind… that ripped
  The gentle world with iron claws. That would amuse me.
  But if a storm comes… It would shred
  The lovely blue eternal sky into a thousand pieces.

Afternoon, Fields and Factory

  I can no longer find a place for my eyes.
  I cannot hold my legs together.
  My heart is hollow. My head is going to burst.
  Mushiness all around. Nothing wants to take shape.
  My tongue breaks. And my mouth twists.
  In my skull there is neither pleasure nor goal.
  The sun, a buttercup, rocks itself
  On a chimney, its slender stalk.

Rainy Night

  The day is ruined. The sky is drunk.
  Like false pearls, little stumps
  Of chopped up light lie around and reveal
  A glimpse of streets, a few clumps of houses.
  Everything else is rotten and devoured
  By a black fog, which, like a wall,
  Falls down and is rotten. And the rain
  Crumbles like rubble in the grip—thick—gray—
  As though the whole contaminated darkness
  Wanted at every moment to sink.
  Down in a swamp you see an auto flash,
  Like a strange, drunken plant.
  The oldest whores come crawling
  Along out of wet shadows—tubercular toads.
  There goes one creeping by. Over there a pig is being stabbed.

The gushing rain wants to wipe out everything.
But you are wandering through the waste lands.
Your dress hangs heavy. Your shoes are soaked.
Your eye is mad with greed and screaming.
And this urges you on—and you have no peace:
Perhaps in the midst of dark fire
The devil himself appears in the form of a pig.
Perhaps something completely horrible,
Foolish, brutal, nasty is happening.

Period

The deserted streets flow in gleaming light
Through my dull head. And hurt me.
I clearly feel that I shall soon slip away—
Thorny roses of my skin, don't prick like that.
The night grows moldy. The poison light of the lampposts
Has smeared it with green muck.
My heart is like a bag. My blood freezes.
The world is dying. My eyes collapse.

Reflecting upon a Human Lung in Alcohol

Without horror you devour dead flesh every day.
And dead blood is a sweet syrup for you.
Aren't you afraid?—
Indeed your earliest fathers also had,
And before you awoke,
Crammed thousands of the dead into your body.

However, how deeply frightened must the first person who killed
An animal have been—
Because, when he saw that what roamed about,
What could jump and cry out and in the moment of death
Still could watch the beseeching world,
In a moment
Was not there.

In the Tuberculosis Sanitarium

Many sick people are walking in the garden
Back and forth and lying in the porches.
Those who are the sickest burn with fever
Every wretched day in the hot
Grave of their beds.
Ah, Catholic sisters float
Around wearily in black clothes.

Yesterday someone died. Today another can die.
In the city Fasching is being celebrated.
I would like to be able to play the difference
On the piano.

Signs

The hour moves forward.
The mole moves out.
The moon emerges furiously.
The ocean heaves.
The child becomes an old man.
Animals pray and flee.
It's getting too hot for the trees.
The mind boggles.
The street dies.
The stinking sun stabs.
The air becomes scarce.
The heart breaks.
The frightened dog keeps its mouth shut.
The sky lies on its wrong side.
The tumult is too much for the stars.
The carriages take off.

The End

Like a white fungus, a lump of wind covers
The green corpse of the lost world.
Frozen rivers form an iron dam
Which holds together the rotten remains.
In a small rainy corner stands
The last city in stony patience.
A dead skull lies—like a prayer—
Slanted on the body, the black penitential bench.

My End

Half hands hold my fate.
Where will it sink…
My steps are tiny, like those of a woman.
One evening lay waste all dreams.
Sleep does not come to me—

Song of Kuno Kohn's Longing

The folds of the sea crash like whips on my skin.
And the stars of the sea tear me apart.

The evening of the sea is one of screaming wounds for the lonely,
But lovers find the good death of their day dreams…
Be there soon, you with pain in your eye, the sea hurts.
Be there soon, you who suffer in love, the sea is killing me.
Your hands are cool saints. Cover me with them,
The sea is burning on me.
But why don't you help me! But help!… Cover me. Save me.
Cure me, friend and woman.
Mother… you—

Invasion

Decline already—
But that was quick…
Hardly a trace of rising—
I have grown above the whole world.
I have become the complete God
And horribly awake.
And now I must cast away death.
My death is mute
And without images…
Without redemption—

Pathos

You don't love me… I have never appealed to you…
Was never your type…
And my hard eyes annoy you, my darling…
I'm too dark for you. And too coarse—
And my white teeth have such a brutal shine
And my bloody lips are so terribly like sickles.
Ah, what you say—
Yes you are really right. I set you… free.
… And early in the morning I am going to an ocean
That is blue and eternal…
And lie on the beach…
And play with a smile on my face, until a death grabs me,
With sand and sun and with a white
Slender bitch.

Love Song

Your eyes are bright lands.
Your looks are little birds,
Handkerchiefs gently waving goodbye.
In your smile I rest as though in bobbing boats.

Your little stories are made of silk.
I must behold you always.

The Suicide

White, I lie
On the remains of an amusement park
Between jagged buildings—
Burning flower... shining sea...
Toes and hands
Reach out into emptiness.
Longing tears the weeping body to pieces.
The little moon glides above me.
Eyes grope
Gently into the deep world,
Sunken hats
Wandering stars.

Touched

I gladly left
The noisy death of the city,
With its thousands of leering faces,
The yellow night of the alleys.
I stride into the broad,
Silver sky;
The pious limbs glide
Deep into gently being.
I am in the white brightness
Of cloud, meadow, wind.
Am tree, am town, am child...
How wet are my eyes!
Soon the green evening will stand
At its silver end...
I raise blessed hands—
I want to go to meet it—

Prayer to People

I go through the days
Like a thief.
And no one hears
My heart lament to itself.
Please have pity.
Like me.

I hate you.
I want to embrace you.

Wanderer in the Evening

Kuno Kohn sings:
Dusty Sunday
Lies burned to pieces.
Charred coolness
Mothers the land.
Dissolute longing
Gapes once again.
Dreams and tears
Stream upward.

Evening

Houses stand stiffly next to their fences.
Let your eyes, last sparrows, flutter.
Bluebottles alight on your face.
Don't you, Kuno, feel the eternal mills—
The unfeeling one bores holes in your head.
Look once more at the moon, the mustard-pot murderer.

Spring

All men are now greedy,
All women are shouting,
Hide yourself in your hump,
Remain alone—

Kuno Kohn's Five Songs to Mary

First Song:

So many years I sought you, Mary—
In gardens, rooms, cities and mountains,
In dumps, whores, in acting schools,
In sick beds and in the rooms of mad people,
In kitchen maids, screaming, celebrations of spring,
In every kind of weather and every kind of day,
In coffee houses, mothers, dancers—
I did not find you in bars, motion pictures,
Music-cafes, excursions into the summer mist...
Who knows the agony, when I, in the night on the streets,
Cried out for you to the dead sky—

Next Song:

He who looks for you in this way, Mary, becomes quite gray.
He who looks for you in this way, Mary, loses his face and legs.
The heart crumbles. Blood and dream escape.
If I could rest… if I were in your hands…
Oh, if you would take me up in your eyes…

Song of Praise

Mary you—to think of how
I felt about you… my heavy head sinks—
Sea only and moon—sea-moon and wind and world—
White sand encircling your white skin, Mary—
Your hair… your smile—all around is sea and distress
And shouts and longing and a gentle happiness—
All this singing, that makes for such weariness…
Doesn't heaven come to us slowly like a mother's song
To the forehead of her child again and again—

Sad Song

Now I go once again among days, animals,
Rocks and thousands of eyes and sounds—
The most foreign one. I had to lose you…
Your sinful body, Mary, was so lovely—
Now I once again in vain look among days, animals,
Rocks and sounds for a trace of you.
Now I also know: I had to lose you…
I did not find you—it was only your name—

Last Song

Only come, my rain… fall against my face
Yellow street lamps… overturn the houses—
I don't want unbroken, smooth roads.
Now it is lovely… only in the light of street lamps…
Mary… surrounded with dark rain—
This is the way it should be. I would like to be with you.
What are mountains and the flat land to me—
What are cities to me and colorful hypnotic nights—
Back to the ocean… back to the starry shore.
You are not entirely Mary, whom I sought.
But you are also Mary—boundless…
Beloved… a fool… cursed with longing…

Kuno's Nocturne

Every day, when it gets so very dark
That I can read no more,
I walk along the street singing,
Look at every girl...
Whether perhaps—who knows—
Today of all days a miracle will take place:
That I shall come home redeemed,
Peaceful and forever free...
From such pursuits I come back
To the house tired and confused,
I know a secret remedy
That can extinguish all suffering—

Going for a Walk

Evening comes with moonshine and silky darkness.
The roads become weary. The narrow world widens.
Winds of opium move in and out of the field.
I widen my eyes like silver wings.
I feel as though my body were the whole earth.
The city lights up: thousands of street lamps sway.
Now the sky also piously enkindles its candlelight.
... Huge above everything my human face wanders—

Ash Wednesday

Yesterday I still went powdered and addicted
Into the many-colored sounding world.
Today everything has long since drowned.
Here is a thing.
There is a thing.
Something seems like this.
Something seems otherwise.
How easily someone blows out
The whole flowering earth.
The sky is cold and blue.
Or the moon is yellow and flat.
A forest has many individual trees.
There's nothing more to cry about.
There's nothing more to scream about.
Where am I—

The Son

Mother, don't hold me,
Mother, your caress hurts me,

See through my face,
How I glow and wane.
Give the last kiss. Let me go.
Send a prayer after me.
That I broke your life,
Mother, forgive me.

To Frida

(Dedicated to L.L.)

Walls separate us.
Strange spider webs.
But I often fly, gaunt in my sinking
Hand wringing room, a bleeding chirping twit.
If only you were there.
I am so murdered.
Frida.

Lonely Watchman

City and beloved are far behind.
I am so betrayed and alone.
Slowly I move from one
Leg to the other.
Around me strange doors screech.
I reach for dagger and gun.
Ah, if I were only at home
With my mother.

Soldiers' Songs

1

It's good and beautiful to be a soldier for a year.
You live longer that way. And one is certainly pleased
With each scrap of time that one snatches from death.
This poor brain, shredded by longing for the city,
Bloody from books, bodies, evenings,
Inconsolably sad and filled with every sin,
Three quarters destroyed already—can only,
Standing at attention and marching on parade,
Swinging arms and legs,
Rust gently in a corner of the skull.
Oh, the stink in a marching column.
Oh, speed-marching across a lovely land in the spring.

2

I must come one hour before the others,
Because I have shot badly.
I certainly won't be promoted.
And I must do extra drills as punishment,
Because, while the others, in accordance with orders,
Looked steadily at the caps of those in front of them,
As we were marching under the red sun
Across the shining fields,
I squinted carefully at the little pilot
Who was humming above me like a bee
In the glowing evening sky.

3

I know, I know; this life is healthy.
My rifle drill is hardly heard,
But I cut my hand badly.
Instead of the damned barracks yard
I could now be in a meadow.
In front of the assembled troops a man begins
To cry bitterly.

4

Sometimes I am afraid: a year is long,
Endlessly long. And always legs swinging...
The whole lovely day spent molding bodies
And parade marching, and firing blanks.
To have to forget the world... that in the evening
One is still senseless, drinking beer, when one goes to sleep
One still feels the heavy helmet on his forehead—
And at night dreams of sergeants—

5

Even when Sundays and evenings come,
Completely empty and listless I move about,
I am completely glassy-eyed, play with dogs for fun,
Ah, or with little stones that I find,
Weary, without a thought, drag myself through the streets.
I often also stand around at my window,
At loose ends; should I just hang out at the local bar
With my dull comrades, kill my weary
Miserable hours in flickering movie houses
And, to pass the time of day
Look for willing girls: or should I merely

Go back and forth in my room.
I, who ran through the nights like a fool,
Shrieking to the sky, sought a thousand miracles.

Songs to Berlin

1

O you Berlin, you colorful stone, you beast.
You cast me with street lamps like briars.
Ah, when one flows in the night through your lamps
After women, silky, plump.
A man gets dizzy from the eye-play.
The little moon-candy sweetens the sky.
When the days struck the steeples.
The head still glows, a red Chinese lantern.

2

Soon I must leave you, my Berlin.
Must again travel into the desolate cities.
Soon I shall sit on the distant hill tops.
In dense woods carve your name.
Farewell, Berlin, with your bold fires.
Farewell, your streets full of adventures.
Who has known as much as I have of your pain.
Saloons, you, I press you to my breast.

3

In meadows and in pure winds peacefully
Cheerful people may glide along gleefully.
We, however, rotten and poisoned long ago,
Would deceive ourselves with this stepping into heaven
In strange cities I move about without direction.
The strange days are hollow and like chalk.
You, my Berlin, you opium rush, you bastard.
Only he who knows longing knows what I suffer.

Monday in the courtyard of the barracks

The heat sticks closely to the gun and to the hand.
It pricks the eyes. Nothing remained forgotten.
The troops stepped, half drunk, into the fire.
The non-coms stand rigidly in front.
The glaring earth is a dead carousel.
Nothing stirs. No one drops down. No streaked sky flies.
Only rarely a hoarse barking tears apart the blue sow

Which lies on the stone barracks.
Now the army leaves me alone.
Who still pays attention to me. They got used
To my strange civilian eyes long ago.
On maneuvers I am half dreaming,
And as we march I compose poems.

But war comes. There was peace too long.
No more good times. Trumpets screech
Deep into your heart. And all the nights are burning.
You freeze in tents. You're hot. You're hungry.
You drown. Explode. Bleed to death. Fields rattle noisily.
Church towers fall. Flames in the distance.
Winds twitch. Large cities crash.
On the horizon cannons thunder.
Around the hill tops a white vapor rises,
And grenades burst at your head.

Now of course

Now of course I put on my straw hat.
Rain has washed the evening blue.
How the world glows! I look up piously,
My hands deep in my trouser pockets.
If the morning drives me home with screams and stones,
Half dead, stripped of my skin,
Yet I'm ready for the night! I shall soon be happy!
Street lamps blaze. Kitchen maids screech!

Elegant Morning

The street looks like eternal Sunday.
Lightly summerhouse rests against summerhouse.
Chauffeurs wheel by grandly.
Three fine citizens glide by quietly.
A song flies coolly out a window.
From a distance the wind carries a child's shout.
And in front of the villa of a duke stands,
All dressed up, like a stiff doll,
In a brightly colored scarf, red as a poppy,
The royal Bavarian legal apprentice,
Doctor of Jurisprudence Kuno Kohn.

Farewell

It sure was fine to be a soldier for a year.
But it is finer to feel free again.

There was enough of depravity and pain
In these merciless human mills.
Sergeants, Barrack walls, farewell.
Farewell canteens, marching songs.
Lighthearted, I leave the city and capitol.
Kuno is leaving, Kuno is never coming back.
Now, fate, drive me where you will.
I am not tugging on my jacket from now on.
I lift my eyes into the world.
A wind is starting up. Locomotives roar.

Farewell

(Shortly before departing for the theater of war)

for Peter Scher

Before dying I am making my poem.
Quiet, comrades, don't disturb me.
We are going off to war. Death is our cement.
If only my beloved did not shed these tears for me.
What am I doing. I go gladly.
Mother is crying. One must be made of iron.
The sun sinks to the horizon.
Soon I shall be tossed into a gentle mass grave.
In the sky the fine red of evening is burning.
Perhaps in thirteen days I'll be dead.

Romantic Journey

Thousands of stars twinkle in the gentle sky.
The landscape glows. From the distant meadow
Mute marching men slowly come closer.
Only once a young Lieutenant, a page boy in love,
Steps out—and stands lost in thought.
The baggage train waddles along at the rear.
The moon makes everything much stranger.
And now and then the drivers cry out:
Stop!
High up on the shakiest munitions truck,
Like a little toad, finely chiseled
Out of black wood, hands gently clenched,
On his back the rifle, gently buckled,
A smoking cigar in his crooked mouth,
Lazy as a monk, needy as a dog
—He had pressed drops of valerian on his heart—

In the yellow moon, ridiculously mad,
Kuno sits.

Warrior's Longing

I would like to lie in my bed
In a white shirt,
Wished the beard was gone,
The head combed.
The fingers were clean,
The nails also,
You, my tender woman,
Might provide peace.

Prayer before Battle

The troops are singing fervently, each for himself:
God, protect me from misfortune,
Father, Son and Holy Spirit,
That no grenades strike me,
That the bastards, our enemies,
Do not catch me, do not shoot me,
That I don't die like a dog
For the dear fatherland.
Look, I would like to go on living,
Milk cows, bang girls
And beat the bastard, Sepp,
Get drunk often
Until my blessed death.
Look, I eagerly and gladly recite
Seven rosaries daily,
If you, God, in your grace
Would kill my friend Huber or Meier,
And not me.
But if the worst should come,
Let me not be too badly wounded.
Send me a slight leg wound,
A small injury to the arm,
So that I may return as a hero,
With a story to tell.

The Grenade

First a bright, brief drum roll,
A bang and explosion into the blue day.
Then a noise, like rockets climbing on

Iron rails. Fear and long silence.
Then suddenly in the distance smoke and a fall,
A strange hard dark echo.

After Combat

In the sky the howitzers no longer explode,
The cannoneers rest next to their guns.
The infantry pitch tents now,
And the pale moon slowly rises.
On yellow fields in red trousers, the French are ablaze,
Ashen pale from death and powder.
Among them German medics squat.
The day becomes grayer, its sun redder.
Field kitchens steam. Towns are put to the torch.
Broken carts stand at roadsides.
Panting cyclists, hot and tanned, loiter
At a scorched wooden fence.
And orderlies are already moving
From regiment to division.

The Battle at Saarburg

The earth grows moldy in fog.
The evening is as oppressive as lead.
Electric sparks crackle and whimper all around,
Breaking everything in two.
Like wretched hobos
Cities are smoking on the horizon.
I lie, God-forsaken,
In the rattling front line of defenders.
Many copper enemy birds
Buzz around heart and brain.
I stand firm in the grayness
And defy death.

Milton Keynes UK
Ingram Content Group UK Ltd.
UKHW020825231024
450026UK00004B/395